Use ProjectLibre

THOMAS ECCLESTONE

ISBN: 1508498881
ISBN-13: 978-1508498889

NONFICTION BOOKS BY AUTHOR

APPLICATION GUIDES
Celestia 1.6 Beginners Guide
Use Opera: The Internet Browser

DOCUMENT PRODUCTION
Use Magix Photo Designer: A Beginners Guide
Use Scribus: The Desk Top Publishing Program

OFFICE PRODUCTIVITY
Use LibreOffice Writer: A Beginners Guide
Use LibreOffice Impress: A Beginners Guide
Use LibreOffice Base: A Beginners Guide
Use LibreOffice Calc: A Beginners Guide

COMPANY MANAGEMENT SOFTWARE
Use Podio: To Manage A Small Company
Use ProjectLibre: for Project Management

CONTENTS

DEDICATION

This book is dedicated to my father for everything he has done.

1 FIRST STEPS WITH PROJECTLIBRE

Why Use ProjectLibre

ProjectLibre is a free open source project management suite that can:

- Help you break down and manage tasks
- Manage resources and costs
- Give you a graphical representation of the progress of a project and,
- Provide a low cost project management solution.

One of the best features of the program is that it provides you with the ability to produce baselines and compare the progress of the project with the original schedule.

It is also a very simple and easy to use piece of software that is ideal for small projects where commercial project management suites are overkill.

First Steps with ProjectLibre

How to download the installer.

Since ProjectLibre is open source software most people

download it from a source repository like SourceForge/. The first step is to go to google and search for the software:

Google will show you a link to download it. Click on the link.

ProjectLibre | SourceForge.net
sourceforge.net/**projects/projectlibre/** ▾
★★★★⋆ Rating: 4.5 - 70 votes - Free - BSD, Linux, Mac OS, Unix, Windows
Download ProjectLibre. The open source replacement of Microsoft Project. ...
ProjectLibre Icon. ProjectLibre. 1 of 5 2 of 5 3 of 5 4 of 5 5 of 5 (70) Read Reviews ...
Download projectlibre-1.5... - Files - Reviews - Support

Your browser address bar will look something like this:

Obviously, since it is a web page the appearance can change over time. But there should be a download button that you can click.

Sourceforge will take you to a web page where the download will start automatically. In Chrome you will see a download status indicator at the bottom of the screen. The download will progress over a reasonable amount of time so it might be worth taking the opportunity to make a nice cup of coffee.

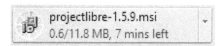

How to run the installer.

When the software finishes downloading you can either click on the box to run it (in chrome) or go to the downloads folder and double click on it there:

Once the installer starts you'll see a setup dialogue:

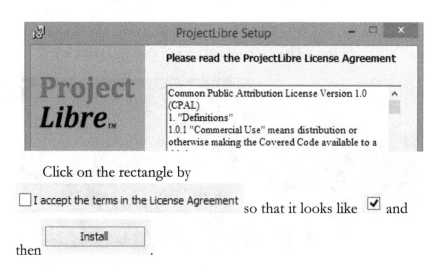

Click on the rectangle by

☐ I accept the terms in the License Agreement so that it looks like ☑ and

then Install .

You'll see a progress bar:

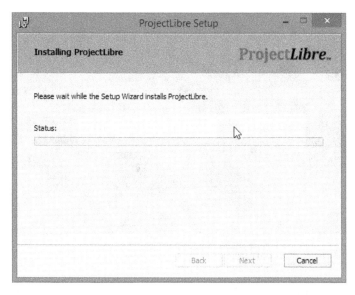

You'll may also see a windows account control dialogue asking if you want to make changes to your computer. Click "Yes" if you see this warning. Once you've agreed that you can make changes the software will install itself. This process doesn't generally take too long. When it's completed you'll see a confirmation message:

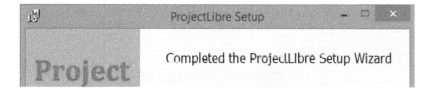

And you should then press [Finish] to close the installer.

In Windows 8.1 to run ProjectLibre click on the windows key, and then search. Type the name of the application into the search bar:

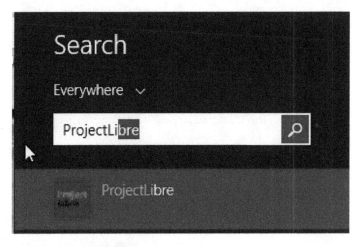

And then click on it:

The first time you run the software you'll see a licensing dialogue. Read the license and if you agree with it click I Accept . Enter your email into the box provided to register the software:

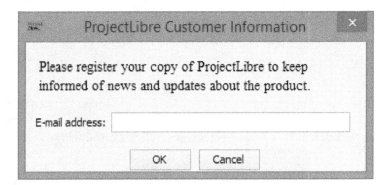

And click OK . You may see a Tip of the Day (the exact tip may vary depending on what the developers want you to know, and the version of the software that you have installed):

Click on [Close] to close the tip of the day. You can also toggle off the [✔] Show tips on startup feature by clicking on the [✔] so it shows [ ]. While you are learning the software I don't recommend that you turn off the tip of the day but it's up to you.

A New Project

Now that you've installed ProjectLibre you'll be given the choice between starting a new project and opening an existing Project. Clearly because it's the first time you've used ProjectLibre I'm going to assume that you're going to [Create Project] although it's always possible that you may want to import an existing project from another piece of software. If you want to import another project I'll explain how to later in the book.

When you create a new project the [New Project] dialogue will be displayed. The first step is to name the new project:

Project Name: Opening Publishing Business

A Project Manager is the person that is responsible for the

project. He or she creates tasks, assigns them to staff members, and may update the schedules and deliverables of the project.

You enter the name of the Manager in the next box:

Manager: Thomas Ecclestone

And the Date that the Project will start:

Start Date: 26/01/15

One thing to consider is if you have already done work prior to using ProjectLibre you may wish to back schedule work. This isn't really an "approved" practice but in the real world it is often done. If so, use a Start Date Prior to the current date and toggle off

☑ Forward scheduled   (click on the ☑ so it shows ☐.)

The final field to fill in is the Notes field. This can be used to give the project a short, easy to understand summary.

Notes:

This is a tutorial for my book "Use ProjectLibre". In it I am going to set basic, simple milestones.

Once you're happy with the settings that you've chosen click   OK   .

The Opening Screen

When you are creating a project for the first time the opening screen in ProjectLibre can seem quite confusing. There's quite a lot going on. It is divided into several main parts.

Tab Bar

The tab bar is where you decide which of the main tasks that you're going to be working on with the software. At first you'll be in the Task tab, which allows you to create project deliverables and milestones.

The File tab allows you to save your project, open another project and so on.

The Resource tab is mainly a method of defining the people that work in your project. You can assign people to particular tasks for a particular duration.

The View tab allows you to display the data in lots of different ways. For example, using different charts and diagrams. You can also filter data so that you see only the information that you need at any one time.

The View Icons

These icons are at the right hand corner of the screen. You can click on them to show additional sections on the screen that display information that you might want while managing the project.

For example  shows the task usage information.

When you want this additional information click on the icon, and if you stop wanting the information click on it a second time to toggle it off.

I'll obviously go into more details about this later in the book.

Task Toolbar:

Each of the main tabs (File, View, Task, and Resource) has a different toolbar. The first toolbar you'll see is the Task Toolbar.

Network	Zoom In	Copy	Insert	Indent	Link	Information	Assign Resources	Find
WBS	Zoom Out	Cut	Delete	Outdent	Unlink	Calendar	Save Baseline	Scroll To Task
Gantt	Task Usage	Paste				Notes	Clear Baseline	Update
Views		Clipboard			Task			

Clicking on options in the toolbar allows you carry out common functions for the tab. For example, you can cut, copy and paste using buttons from the toolbar.

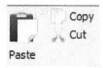

Main Work Area:

Below the toolbar for each tab you'll see the main work area. Each tab (and often, within the same tab each view and task you're carrying out) will display a different screen.

Below is the Gantt view for the Task tab.

	Name	Duration	Start	26 Jan 15	2 Feb 15	9 Fe
				F S S M T W T F S S	M T W T F S S	M h

While this section of the book has given you only a very brief overview you shouldn't be too worried. I'll explain in detail how to use a lot of the functionality you're seeing. But in this section of the book I only want to create a small project to get you to the point that you can use the most essential parts of the software quickly.

Thoughts about tasks.

Everyone has come across tasks in their real life. A task is something that you have to do, by a deadline, by someone with a deliverable (i.e. with something that the task will achieve.)

A simple task might be "Make a cup of coffee".

A more complicated task is often called a project, for example "Build a house." Each task or project can be broken down to smaller units (tasks and subtasks):

Build a house

   Make Building Plans

      Hire an Architect

      Make Drawings

      Cost Drawings

   Put through Planning Permission

      Apply

      Advertise / Notify planning application

      Attend planning permission meeting

   Carry out Building Work

      Hire a Builder

      Hire a Building Project Manager

   Sign off with building inspector

   Report to council

The main task "Build a house" is so complicated that we call it a project. Subtasks like Make Building Plans are still very complicated and so we break them down into subtasks.

The reality is that even huge projects like "Manned mission to mars" can be broken down in this way until each of the subtasks are small enough so they can be accomplished. Project management is largely a matter of making sure that you break tasks down until they are small enough that you can work out how they will progress.

Agile Project Management

One of the things that has happened in the past is that people get bogged down quite a lot at the planning stage. Instead of thinking of project management as a one-off task it's generally very important to set up a process of continuous monitoring, adjustment, and review. So that as the project continues and you learn more about what it requires you revisit the plan on a regular basis.

Project management often involves trial and error.

Starting a Project: Resources vs Tasks.

People do have different approaches to designing a project. Lots of people decide to create Tasks first and then add people (resources) when they've decided what needs to happen to accomplish goals. But other people choose to add resources first because they are constrained and so it's easiest to add them.

This depends to an extent on the size of the project and your own company since often in small companies the people that you have available are very limited and so it only makes sense to design tasks that correlate with what individuals can do.

In this tutorial I'm going to use a "Task First" approach to creating a project.

Adding a New Task

To create a task make sure that you are in the task Tab:

| File | Task | Resource | View |

It helps if you're in the GANTT view, which by default you should be the first time that you use the software. Below the Task toolbar you should see the following:

If you have used the software before so you're in a different view click on Gantt to go into the GANTT view.

To create your first step click on the Name field and type in a name:

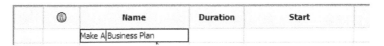

Click into the next box, the duration box, and type a number such as 1h (for 1 hour), 1d (for 1 day), or 1 y. for 1 year. I find that it's generally better to use decimal places to refer to parts of days rather than h. For example:

Once you've added a duration (remember to click off to a new line), ProjectLibre will automatically calculate the Start and Finish dates for you. These will show up in the Start and Finish fields, but they will also be displayed on the Gantt chart as below:

		Name	Duration	Start		26 Jan 15	2 Feb 15
1		Opening Publishing Business	4 days	26/01/15 08:00	29/0		

Insert a new Task Above an existing Task

It's pretty common to have new ideas while you're working out the project plan. In fact, that's one of the best reasons to do it! Simply working on one part of the plan will often suggest things that you have to do before the current task.

To insert the task above another task, select the other task by clicking on the number at the left hand side of the list:

When you've select a task you'll see that it is highlighted:

ⓐ	Name	Duration	Start
1	Opening Publishing Business	4 days	26/01/15 08:00

Then click  in the toolbar. You'll see a new line above the current task:

1	Opening Publishing Business	4 days 26/01/15 08:00		2S

As above, click on the Name field and type a name, then on the duration field and type a duration:

Changing the Start Date for a Task

ProjectLibre is often, well, a little optimistic about when you'll be able to start a task. It'll assume that you're raring to get going and if the task isn't liked to another task it'll by default start it right away.

To change the start day click into the start field:

Name	Duration	Start	
Register for tax	0.2 days	26/01/15 08:00 ‍I ▼	26

Then click on the arrow ▼ to show the calendar:

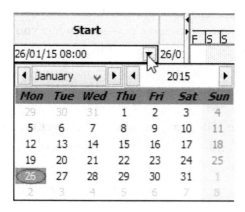

This works as expected. You can change the month by clicking

on the arrows to move backwards or forwards  or
the same with the month: .

Once you're in the right month or year click on the day.

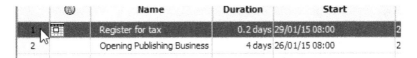

This can have more effects than it seems at first. Sometimes you have "linked tasks" where one task can only begin when another ends. If this is the case, changing a predecessor task will have effects on later tasks.

I'll explain this in more detail later.

Delete a task

Select the task by clicking on the number again.

	ⓐ	Name	Duration	Start	
1		Register for tax	0.2 days	29/01/15 08:00	2
2		Opening Publishing Business	4 days	26/01/15 08:00	2

In the tasks toolbar, click on ⬤ Delete .

Using Cut, Copy and Paste

Say you have a lot of tasks already created:

	ⓐ	Name	Duration	Start	
1		Opening Publishing Business	4 days	26/01/15 08:00	29/0
2		Write Business Plan	2 days	26/01/15 08:00	27/0
3		Market Business	10 days	26/01/15 08:00	06/0
4		Hire Editing Staff	1 day	26/01/15 08:00	26/0
5		Publish Books	4 days	26/01/15 08:00	29/0

You suddenly realise that it's a pretty silly idea to write the business plan (task 2) before you open the business (task 1). How do you move it so the task is in the right place?

One of the easiest ways to do it is to select the task you want to move (click on the number)

	Ⓐ	Name	Duration	Start	
1		Opening Publishing Business	4 days	26/01/15 08:00	29/0
2		Write Business Plan	2 days	26/01/15 08:00	27/0
3		Market Business	10 days	26/01/15 08:00	06/0

Cut it by pressing ✂ Cut in the toolbar:

	Ⓐ	Name	Duration	Start	
1		Opening Publishing Business	4 days	26/01/15 08:00	29/0
2		Market Business	10 days	26/01/15 08:00	06/0
3		Hire Editing Staff	1 day	26/01/15 08:00	26/0
4		Publish Books	4 days	26/01/15 08:00	29/0

Then select the task that you want to move it to:

	Ⓐ	Name	Duration	Start	
1		Opening Publishing Business	4 days	26/01/15 08:00	29/0
2		Market Business	10 days	26/01/15 08:00	06/0

And press Paste :

1		Write Business Plan	2 days	26/01/15 08:00	27/0
2		Opening Publishing Business	4 days	26/01/15 08:00	29/0

Obviously, cut works the same way you'd expect if you've used it in other applications like word processors. Copy (Copy in the toolbar) also works in the way you'd expect. It takes a copy which you can then paste as above but it leaves the original intact.

Creating a Subtask

I've already described subtasks above. While a task is quite a large unit of effort a subtask is a smaller one that you need to complete in order to complete a task.

To make something into a subtask in the Gantt view you've got to indent it. You can either do it by selecting one task at a time, or select multiple tasks by going to the left hand corner, clicking on the first number that you want to select, then moving the mouse down to the last number you want to select:

	ⓘ	Name	Duration	Start	
1		Write Business Plan	2 days	26/01/15 08:00	27/0
2		Opening Publishing Business	4 days	26/01/15 08:00	29/0
3		Market Business	10 days	26/01/15 08:00	06/0
4		Hire Editing Staff	1 day	26/01/15 08:00	26/0
5		Publish Books	4 days	26/01/15 08:00	29/0

Visually in ProjectLibre you'll see that a subtask is indicated through indentation. So to make a task into a subtask press ▶ Indent :

1		Write Business Plan	2 days	26/01/15 08:00	27/0
2		⊟ Opening Publishing Busin	10 days	26/01/15 08:00	06/0
3		Market Business	10 days	26/01/15 08:00	06/0
4		Hire Editing Staff	1 day	26/01/15 08:00	26/0
5		Publish Books	4 days	26/01/15 08:00	29/0

Visually, you see that the main task becomes bold on the diagram. There's another impact of these subtasks. The duration you specified is overridden by the duration of the subtasks. So, if the subtasks take 10 days in total to complete you'll see that duration of the main task is 10 days).

Also, the Gantt chart will change too, to reflect the fact that there is a task with subtasks. A task that has subtasks is displayed using a ▼▬▬▬▬▬▬▼ symbol.

A task that doesn't have subtasks is displayed as a coloured bar: ▬▬ .

For example:

⊟ Opening Publishing Busin	10 days	26/01/15 08:00	06/(
Market Business	10 days	26/01/15 08:00	06/0:
Hire Editing Staff	1 day	26/01/15 08:00	26/0

Tasks scheduled before the current date.

So far we have used very simple examples for our project. As the project carries on you'll have tasks that were scheduled to start before the current date. See the following:

	Write Business Plan	1 day	23/01/15 08:00	23/0
	Get Finance	3 days	26/01/15 08:00	28/0
	Hire Manager	5 days	26/01/15 08:00	30/0

The Project start date is indicated by a dotted line. You can also see the current date which is displayed in light green.

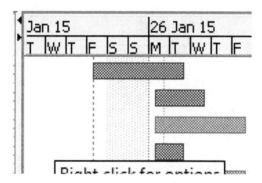

In the above example, I've got a task that starts before the current date and time. This allows you to see tasks that (should) have already started.

Reporting Progress

So far we've just created tasks. But one of the most common things that a project manager needs to do is assess the progress that they have made towards a task. You can do this by changing the progress marker for the task.

Double click on the number at the left hand side of the task. This will bring up the Task Information dialogue for that task.

This dialogue contains a lot of information, but one of the most important fields is the percentage complete.

Percent Complete: 0%

Change it to a number, such as 60% (or however complete the task is) then click on   Close   .

Note that inside the progress bar you'll see a bold line. This line indicates how complete it is. If the progress line is ahead of the green "current date" line it means that the task is ahead of schedule.

Progress indicators can be used to give the project manager a good idea about whether the project is on schedule or not.

Deliverables and Milestones

So far I've talked extensively about tasks, but nothing about deliverables which is the outcome of a task. All tasks should have deliverables attached to them. For example, the task "Writing a first draft" will have the first draft book as the deliverable.

Creating a deliverable is actually pretty simple. You just set the duration to 0 days.

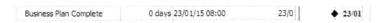

Note that the icon changes to a diamond.

Once you've done this you've got to consider whether the deliverable is actually a milestone. A milestone denotes the finish of a stage of the project. For example, in a project to start a business the business plan might be a milestone, but producing a profit and loss account might be considered just a deliverable.

To turn a deliverable into a milestone, double click on the number to open the task information dialogue.

In the dialogue click on the Advanced tab. Notice there is an

option to ☐ Display task as milestone . Toggle it on:

✔ Display task as milestone then press Close .

Linking Tasks

So far we have used only unlinked tasks. Such tasks don't depend on other tasks being completed. But we can think of a lot of projects where one task depend on the next. For example, when you're making a cup of coffee the task "Boil kettle" comes before "Put water in cup." Until you complete the predecessor task you *can't* complete the next task.

This relationship is called a linked task.

The first step in linking two tasks together is to click on the first task, and then hold the control (often ctrl on keyboards) key and click on the task you want to link to. This will select both tasks:

		Name	Duration	Start		Jan 15	26 Jan 15	2 Feb
1		Write Business Plan	3 days	23/01/15 08:00	27/0			
2		Business Plan Complete	0 days	27/01/15 16:00	27/0	◆ 27/01		
3		Get Finance	3 days	26/01/15 08:00	28/0			
4		Hire Manager	5 days	26/01/15 08:00	30/0			

Then, click on 🔗 Link in the task tab toolbar. There are several things to notice here. The first is that the link relationship is shown by an arrow. And the second thing is that the beginning date of the successor task is moved to after the end of the predecessor task.

		Name	Duration	Start		Jan 15	26 Jan 15	2 Feb 1
1		Write Business Plan	3 days	23/01/15 08:00	27/0			
2		Business Plan Complete	0 days	27/01/15 16:00	27/0	◆ 27/01		
3		Get Finance	3 days	28/01/15 08:00	30/0			
4		Hire Manager	5 days	26/01/15 08:00	30/0			
5		Open for Submissions	2 days	28/01/15 09:00	30/0			

You will often find that some tasks are linked, for example you can't hire the manager until you've got finance. But other tasks can be unlinked. They don't depend on an earlier task. Where one task is running at the same time as another they are called concurrent tasks.

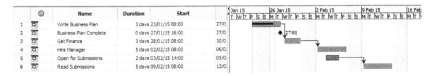

It's possible to link tasks with deliverables and milestones. In fact, as a rule I generally link them together. This makes sure that while you're moving task start dates and duration you will move the milestone at the same time.

Basic File Tasks

ProjectLibre allows you to save, open, close, and save as using the File tab. You'll see that these options are available at the left hand side of the toolbar.

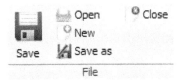

Many of these options are pretty self-explanatory. For example if you hit Open you'll see an open dialogue.

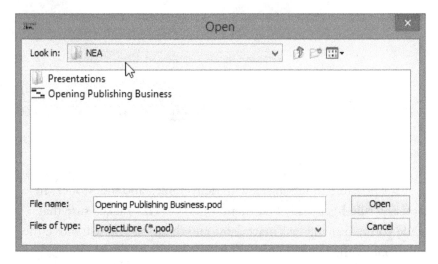

You can control the types of files that ProjectLibre will display in the Open dialogue using the Files of Type dialogue box:

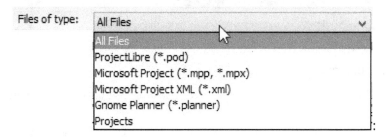

As you can see above you can import Microsoft Project and Gnome Planner projects.

Export File to Microsoft Project

To export a file to Microsoft Project (or change its name, etc.) click on ⊞ Save as . Choose Microsoft Project XML as the format that you want to save using the Files of Type dialogue.

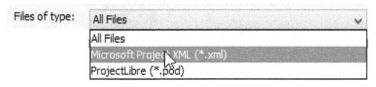

.Choose the file name

File name: | Opening Publishing Business.xml | .and click | Save | .

Switching Between Open Projects

You can open multiple projects by clicking on Open . This will show a standard Open dialogue of the type that you are probably very familiar with.

You can open several Projects at the same time. ProjectLibre doesn't close down a project that you are working on just because you open another project. However, you can only work on one instance of an project at a time (so, if you're working on Company Standards and choose to open it again ProjectLibre will automatically close the version that is currently in memory, asking if you want to save the file before it does so. Then it will open the version that is on the hard disk. If you choose not to save the current version this has the effect of reverting to the old version)

If you are working on multiple files it's often the case that you'll want to switch between them. At the top right hand side of the screen you'll see a little combo box that has the name of the project that you are currently working on.

When you click on it you'll see a list of currently open projects. Click on the project that you want to work on.

Projects

To view and edit a list of currently opened projects click

on Projects in the File tab. The summary table that this displays contains the name, start and finish dates, managers and a lot of other information.

Name	Start	Finish	Manager	Status Date
Opening Publishing Business	23/01/15 08:00	16/03/15 10:00	Thomas Ecclestone	12/02/15 17:00
Company Stadards	12/02/15 08:00	12/02/15 08:00	Eric Bigbos	12/02/15 17:00

Note that you can change the fields that aren't greyed out by clicking onto them.

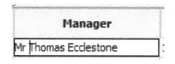

The Greyed out fields are summary fields where the information displayed is calculated automatically when you click Update in the File Tab (or, often, if you save, go to another tab or view).

You can see much of the same information by clicking on Projects Dialog. Instead of a table in the viewable area the information is displayed in a dialogue allowing you to view it while you're working on GANTT charts or resource management.

Project Information

Click on Information in the File Tab to display the project information dialogue. You'll find that this dialogue allows you to change the status of a project as well as the project type, and other information features that may be of use.

Use ProjectLibre

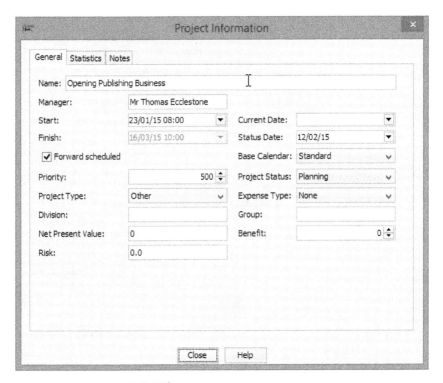

Click on the Statistics tab to display information about the current project:

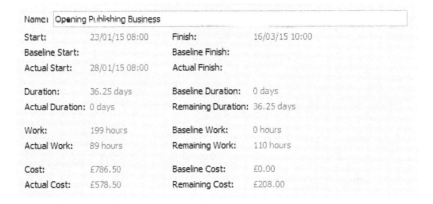

Printing

You can print the content of the current viewable area (i.e.

whatever is beneath the toolbar) from the File tab. Click on

Preview to see the print preview (I routinely advise doing a print preview since it makes it so much easier to see whether you're printing the parts of the document that you want to print).

It will open on the first page of the print preview. You can use the navigation options at the top of the screen to go to the next page or previous page ❮ or the last page or first page .

There are also zoom options (zoom in has the plus symbol, zoom reset, and zoom out with the minus symbol in the centre) to make the preview larger or smaller.

On the right hand side are printer preferences. Firstly, you can click on the combo box under printers to find a list of the currently installed printers on your system:

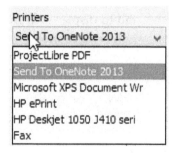

ProjectLibre PDF is a PDF export driver.

The next options allow you to control the format of the printed document. For example, you can control the Layout (Landscape or portrait, although for most reports the default orientation is best) and choose what paper format you're going to use in the printer, and the margins for the document.

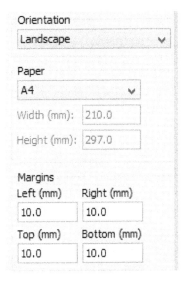

So far most of these options are pretty standard. ProjectLibre also offers you the ability to decide whether to show the table or spreadsheet, and what chart to show (if any). In practice it's often the case that printing out the spreadsheet and the Gantt chart is pretty sensible since otherwise the Gantt can be hard to read.

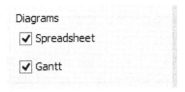

Finally, you can choose what scaling you will apply to the document. The preview can give you a good view of what the final printed document will look like given your scaling choices.

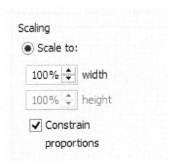

When you have chosen your options click on 🖶 to print the document or 🖼 to export it to PDF. If you export it to PDF you'll see a save dialogue and have to choose a directory and file name in the normal way. Click on [×] to close the print preview if necessary.

Next Chapter

In this chapter I've discussed how to install ProjectLibre, and given some basic information on how to use it.

In the next Chapter I'm going to discuss a related piece of software that can be useful for recording how much time someone spends on a project.

2 USING TIMETRACKER FOR TIME SHEETS

As we saw in the last chapter it's important to record how much time someone has spent on a project. While it's possible to make a spreadsheet or manually record this kind of information there are open source pieces of software that can help when you want to record the amount of time that someone spends at a task.

Installing TimeTracker

To install Oxff Timetracker go to http://0xff.net/site/index.php/timetracker/downloads/ where you'll find the latest version of the installer.

Latest Timetracker version(s):

Timetracker-0.9.11.2.exe   1.97 MB   24-06-2012 21:04

Click on it to download it. When it's finished downloading it should be available in your download folder. Double click on it to launch the installer.

Name	Date modified	Type	Size
Timetracker-0.9.11.2	22/07/2014 13:40	Application	1,926 KB

Click Yes in the User Account Controller dialogue. The installer

splash screen will be displayed. Click [Next >] then [I Agree].
This will open a new screen that allows you to change the destination
folder.

> Destination Folder
>
> [C:\Program Files (x86)\Timetracker\ ]   [Browse...]

Click on [Browse...] to open a browse for folder dialogue.

Once you're happy with your folder click on [Next >]. You
can change the start menu folder, although I don't recommend doing
so.

> Select the Start Menu folder in which you would like to create the program's shortcuts. You
> can also enter a name to create a new folder.
>
> [Timetracker]

Then click on [Install]. You'll see a progress dialogue. It
shouldn't take long. Click on [Finish] to start the time tracker

application. It will start in the background – note that its icon 🏃 will
either appear on the bottom right hand side of the screen near the

calendar or, possibly, be hidden in which case you should press ▲ to
show hidden icons

Either way, click on the icon 🏃 to display the program.

Adding a Project

The first task that you'll have is to add your project. Look at the left hand side of the Timetracker dialogue. You'll see a project section:

Click on Add Projects 🖥 to display the new project dialogue. Then type in the project name

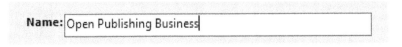

And any notes that you want to add about the project:

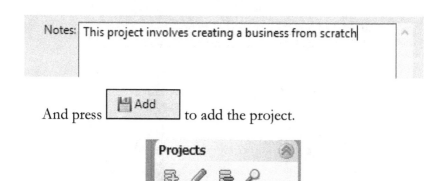

And press  to add the project.

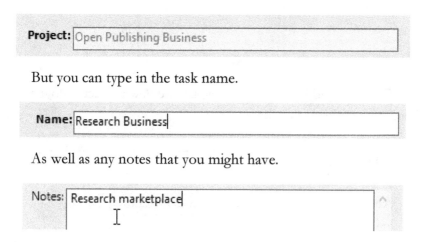

Adding a Task

When you add a new project Time Tracker will automatically create a new task for you. At other times, click on Project that you want to add a task for in the Projects section, and then click on Add Tasks 🖻 under the tasks section.

When you are adding a task you'll see that the Project is already included in the details.

But you can type in the task name.

As well as any notes that you might have.

Then you can click on ⟨Add⟩ to add the task, and

⟨Add & Start⟩ to add the task and then start recording (although I recommend that you add all the tasks for the project when you start using the project rather than doing it on an ad hoc basis).

You'll see that you have now got a project and a task.

When you want to record or edit a task you'll need to select (i.e. click on) the Project first. You can edit a task or project by clicking on it to select it and then clicking ✏ or select a project and task and click on 🖨 to remove it permanently. Note that if you delete a project or task you'll lose all the information that is associated with it. So don't do it unless you're sure.

Recording time on a task

First select the project by clicking on it in the project list:

Then select the task by clicking on it in the task list.

Then click on to start recording. You'll see that the task appears in the time tracking window on the right hand side.

Day	Start Ti...	Stop Ti...	Duration	Project	Task	Details
13/02/2015	12:31	-	00:00:01	Open Publishing Business	Research Busi...	

Duration is an interesting feature. It will keep on increasing until you press to stop recording.

Day	Start Ti...	Stop Ti...	Duration	Project	Task	Details
13/02/2015	12:31	12:32	00:01:16	Open Publishing Business	Research Busi...	

At the bottom left hand of the screen you'll see the duration that you've worked on the task today.

You can click on any of the fields to change them, although clicking on the details column is particularly recommended since it is often hard to remember exactly what you did in the session:

Day	Start Ti...	Stop Ti...	Duration	Project	Task	Details
13/02/2015	12:31	12:32	00:00:34	Open Publishing Business	Research Busin...	Created task

Seeing other days logs

At the top of the screen there is the date that you're currently logging.

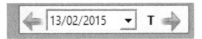

You can click the arrows to go to the previous day  or the next day , or click on the combo box to show a calendar.

Running a Report

You can run a report from the Reports section. There are three main types of report. The Text Report, the Chart, and Table.

I find that to find out how much time has been spent on a project) the text report is best. First select the Project and Task and then click on Text to run the report. At the top of the screen you'll see a section that defines the amount of time the report will be run on. You can find out how much time you've spent on the task during today, this week or this month.

Generally, though, you'll click on 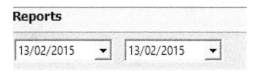 to toggle it on. You'll see the date range at the left hand side of the screen.

Reports

13/02/2015 ▼   13/02/2015 ▼

Click on the first combo box to specify the first day that you were involved in the project:

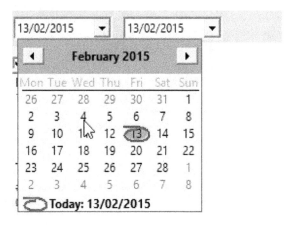

And leave the second combo box on today's date.

12/02/2015 ▼   13/02/2015 ▼

You'll see how much time has been spent on the project:

_Summary (Hours per Project)_____

#Hours   Project
00:05   Open Publishing Business

But... we're not really all that concerned about the time we've spent working on a project. We need to find out how much time we've spent working on each task in the project. And none of the reports seem to provide that information.

Adding the Rich Text Report Plugin

Click on [] to bring up the information window, then on the | Add/Remove Plugins | tab. You'll see a list of currently installed plugins. Click on List available | to open up a list of available plugins in your default browser.

Latest Timetracker version(s):

Timetracker-0.9.11.2.exe   1.97 MB   24-06-2012 21:04

Timetracker Plugins:

GreenWorkingManPlugin.ttp	24.58 kB	03-04-2011 21:29
NoTaskWarningPlugin.ttp	28.67 kB	31-01-2009 15:37
PSPPlugin.ttp	24.58 kB	03-01-2009 17:40
RedWorkingManPlugin.ttp	24.58 kB	03-04-2011 21:30
RichTextReport.ttp	27.14 kB	03-04-2011 21:30
WITPlugin.ttp	32.77 kB	13-01-2009 23:37

Click on

RichTextReport.ttp   27.14 kB   03-04-2011 21:30

to download the rich text report plugin. It'll download to the downloads folder unless you select another folder.

Then press Add... and navigate to the folder that you just downloaded

▶ This PC ▶ Downloads   ∨ ↻ . You should see the plugin in the list of files.

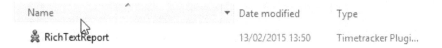

Double click on it to add the plugin. You'll see the plugin appear in the list. It'll have a red circle and a note that you need to restart the program to use the plugin.

Click on 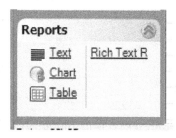. The program will close down and then it will restart. If it starts minimised click on ![icon] at the bottom right hand side of the screen, or in the show hidden icons ![icon] option. You'll see the new report appear in the list.

Click on ![Rich Text R] to run the Rich Text Report. You can adjust the dates of the report in the same way as the Text Report that I showed you earlier.

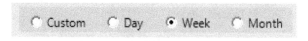

Remember, I suggested using ![Custom] and then setting the start date to the beginning of the project. Once you've chosen the dates the report will run automatically. You'll see a list of Projects that you've worked on during the period, plus how long you worked on the task.

Project	Task	Duration
Open Publishing Business		1:07 [100%]
	Research Business	0:05
	Run ProjectLibre	1:02

Next Chapter

It's important to track time in order to get the most out of the task view in ProjectLibre. While there are a lot of time tracking applications I've shown you a very simple and easy way to automatically record the time that you spend doing a task.

The next chapter will carry on the progress to show how to handle people within the project – or "Resources" as they are known in ProjectLibre.

3 RESOURCES

ProjectLibre people are called "Resources". You assign people to tasks but you can also control project costing through the use of a timesheet facility and show how resources have been utilised in the project.

There are other forms of resources – i.e. material resources – which you may sometimes use as well, but in the vast majority of cases the resources that people generally track are human resources.

Adding a Resource

To manage resources you need to click on the Resource tab.

Then click on Resources . You will see a list of resources that have been employed in your project which is empty at the moment because you haven't added a resource.

⊙	Name	RBS	Type	E-mail Address	Material Label

To add a person to the project type there name into an empty name box:

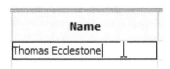

Press the tab key to go to the next field. Ignore RBS for the moment and then click tab and check that the type is "Work". This means that the resource is a person. Tab again to include e-mail, initials (which ProjectLibre sometimes uses to show the person), the company group, the maximum unit percentage, and rates.

Most of these columns are pretty straight forward.

The rate columns (Standard Rate, Overtime Rate, and Cost Per Use) are all used in order to cost the project. If you use 20 hours of time for someone earning £6.50 per hour the cost to the project will be billed at £130.

The accrue at column says when the cost will be billed to the project as work is carried out, or when the persons involvement with the project starts or end for any particular task.

Assigning a Resource to a Task

You need to be in the GANTT view to assign a person to a task.

Click on ^{Task} in the tabs, then ^{Gantt} . Select the task that you want to add the resource to.

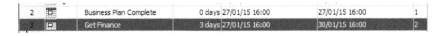

Then, click on Assign Resources in the toolbar. You'll see the Assign Resources dialogue.

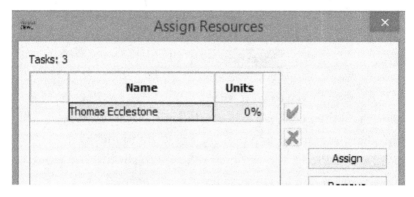

Click onto the units column and type the percentage of that person's time that the task will have on the days that the person works on the project

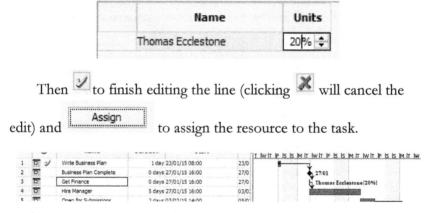

Then ✓ to finish editing the line (clicking ✗ will cancel the edit) and **Assign** to assign the resource to the task.

1		Write Business Plan	1 day 23/01/15 08:00	23/0
2		Business Plan Complete	0 days 27/01/15 16:00	27/0
3		Get Finance	0 days 27/01/15 16:00	27/0
4		Hire Manager	5 days 27/01/15 16:00	03/0
5		Open for Submissions	2 days 03/02/15 14:00	05/0

We see that the task has changed so that it reflect the fact that a person has been assigned to it.

Adding number of hours that a person is going to work on the project

Double click on the task to show the Task Information then click on the Resources tab. You will see the resources that have been assigned to the task.

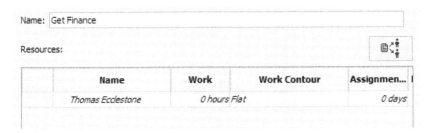

To add a number of hours or days that the resource will work on the project type your number in the work column, using h for hours, d for days, a y for years. For example:

Now, here's something that some people find confusing. You'll see that when you press enter or tab the resource usage will change (naturally) but it will change in a way you don't expect:

Name	Work	Work Contour	Assignment
Thomas Ecclestone	8 hours	Flat	

Yeah. Well, that's a bit of a puzzler at first. But it's because we've assigned the person to the project for 5 days, but he is only working on it for 20% of the day. (The default work day in ProjectLibre is 8 hours. You can change this, and I'll explain how later on).

We also see that the Gantt chart has changed again:

In other words, the task will take 5 days to complete, but our resource will only work on it for 20% of his time.

We can insert more Resources into the project, each with their own individual number of hours:

Name	Work	Work Contour	Assignment
Thomas Ecclestone	8 hours	Flat	
Joe Slow	3.2 hours	Flat	

One thing to watch out for, though, is that it's generally best to assign all the team members (or resources) to a task before you define the work column. This is because if you add a new worker to a project ProjectLibre will automatically try to share the work load evenly between the new project members and the old project members. In other words, the number of hours you've already set will change.

There is also an Assignment Delay and Leveling Delay field that isn't used yet in this version of the software but will be used in the enterprise version that will be released later on.

Replacing a Resource In a task

Warning: before carrying out this task save a backup copy of your project.

Say you've just hired a new worker. You decide Samantha Quick would be better fit for the task than Joe Slow.

		Name	RBS	Type
1		Thomas Ecclestone		Work
2		Joe Slow		Work
3		Samantha Quick		Work

In the Task tab and the Gantt view double click on the task to bring up the Task Information dialogue. In the Resources tab of the dialogue you'll see a list of people that have already been assigned to the task. Click on . When the assign resources dialogue opens up, click on Joe Slow:

Tasks: 3

Name	Units
Thomas Ecclestone	20%
Joe Slow	40%
Samantha Quick	

Then on Replace... .

This will display the Replace Resource dialogue:

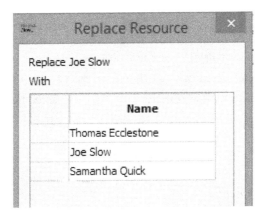

Click on the person you want to replace Joe Slow with:

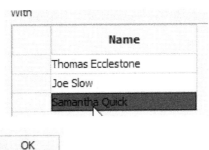

Then Press OK .

You'll see that the allocation list has changed.

Name	Units	
Thomas Ecclestone	20%	✔
Joe Slow		
Samantha Quick	100%	✘

Uh oh! There's a problem with making these kind of changes. As you'll see below, because you've replaced one individual working on the task with another you'll lose the working time you've entered:

Name	Work	Work Contour	Assignment D...
Thomas Ecclestone	0 hours	Flat	1.125 days
Samantha Quick	0 hours	Flat	0 days

This is also a problem for the Remove Resources option. There's not much you can do about it, other than make sure that before you start managing the task you include all the resources that are likely to work on it.

Removing a Resource from a Task

As before go to the Task tab and the Gantt view. Then double click on the task and click on the Resources to see a list of people that have already been assigned to the task.

Name	Work	Work Contour	Assignment D...	Leveling D...	Cost Rate
Thomas Ecclestone	0.423 hours	Flat		1.125 days	0 days	Rate A
Joe Slow	0 hours	Flat		0 days	0 days	Rate A
Samantha Quick	3.176 hours	Flat		0 days	0 days	Rate A

Click on ⬛ to bring up the assign resources dialogue. Click on the resource you want to remove from the task.

Tasks: 3

Name	Units	
Thomas Ecclestone	20%	✓
Joe Slow	50%	✗
Samantha Quick	100%	

Then on [Remove] .

Again, doing this will remove the information that you've already added about the assignment of other resources to the project. You can get around this by allocating a resource to 0 duration for the task although that's not a particularly beautiful approach.

Notes about a Resource

You can record notes about a resource. These notes can be almost anything that is relevant to the resource, for example it can reflect the fact that a resource has particular skills, abilities, or other peculiarities.

In the _Resource_ tab click on _Resources_ to show a list of resources available to the project. Click on the resource that you're interested in.

	ⓐ	Name	RBS	Type
1		Thomas Ecclestone		Work
2		Joe Slow		Work
3		Samantha Quick		Work

Then click on ☰ Notes . You will see the resource information tab open up. You can read notes that you've already added or, alternatively, edit the notes to add more information about the resource.

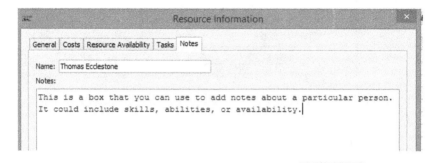

When you're happy with your changes click | Close | .

Showing Resource Allocation

Click on ⊞ to show the resource usage.

Note that ProjectLibre will adjust task length and resource usage as you change the work schedule of particular team members.

	Name	Work	Work Contour	Assign	26 Jan 15				
					M	T	W	T	F
1	Thomas Ecclestone	8 hours		Work	0h	0.2h	1.6h	1.6h	1.6
	Get Finance	8 hours Flat		Work		0.2h	1.6h	1.6h	1.6
2	Joe Slow	3.2 hours		Work	0h	0.4h	2.8h	0h	0
	Get Finance	3.2 hours Flat		Work		0.4h	2.8h		

Because there isn't a levelling function in ProjectLibre yet it is often a good idea to show a histogram of resource usage to check that you haven't overbooked someone. Click on 📊 to see how you've allocated people so far. First click on the name of the person that you want to show the histogram for, for example ◯ Thomas Ecclestone . You'll see the histogram for the specified person:

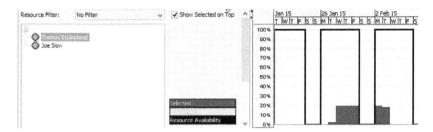

If you try to over allocate someone it should be very obvious by using these two views.

Note also that you can see only the resource usage by clicking on

the  tab, and then Resource Usage

Finding the Project Resource Cost

Well, so far we've given a resource a cost per hour, and we've said that we're going to use a resource for a particular number of hours. It's not rocket science that ProjectLibre can calculate the cost for a particular assignment.

In the 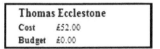 tab click RBS .

Thomas Ecclestone		Joe Slow	
Cost	£52.00	Cost	£25.60
Budget	£0.00	Budget	£0.00

Finding the Task Cost

It's possible to find out the Task Cost by clicking onto the

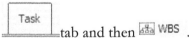 tab and then WBS .

Business Plan Complete			Get Finance		Hire Manager	
Cost	£0.00		Cost	£77.60	Cost	£0.00
Budget			Budget		Budget	

Specifying days when someone isn't working.

Obviously so far we've used a relatively simple scheduling method. We've just assumed that every staff member is full time and that no staff member is going to go on holiday at any point during the project.

The reality is obviously different from that.

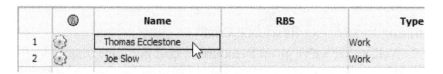

In the Resource tab click on Resources and then double click on the name of the person whose availability you want to change.

	ⓘ	Name	RBS	Type
1		Thomas Ecclestone		Work
2		Joe Slow		Work

This opens the Resource Information dialogue which is very similar to the Task Information dialogue. You can see that one of the options in the General tab is base calendar:

The Base Calendar allows you to choose from three main types of calendars. The first is a standard, office type calendar. The next is a 24 hour calendar where you'll specify part time workers hours, and the third is a night shift calendar.

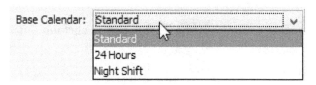

Choosing the most logical calendar is important because it will save time as you're entering data. Obviously it's possible to change these basic calendars but I'll describe how to do that later on.

Once you've chosen a basic calendar, click on change working time 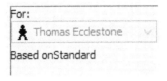. This will bring up a calendar dialogue. On the right hand side it will show a calendar, and on the left it will show the name of the person and what calendar it's based on:

For:

👤 Thomas Ecclestone ⌄

Based onStandard

The first step is to select the days that you want to change. You can select the first one by clicking on it.

January 2015

S	M	T	W	T	F	S
				1	2	3
4	5	6	7	8	9	10
11	12	13	14	15	16	17
18	19	20	21	22	23	24

Then you've got a choice. You can select additional days by either holding down control (ctrl on most keyboards) and clicking additional days, or you can hold shift and go to the end of the range that you want to select. If that's the end of the week, it would look something like this.

January 2015

S	M	T	W	T	F	S
				1	2	3
4	5	6	7	8	9	10
11	12	13	14	15	16	17
18	19	20	21	22	23	24
25	26	27	28	29	30	31

But what happens if you want to select more than one range? Well, go to the beginning of the next range and hold control (ctrl) and click on it.

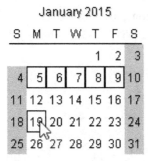

Then, like before, hold the shift key down and click at the end of the range.

Another thing to note is that you can use the arrow keys to edit months that are outside the range of months that ProjectLibre is showing you.

So, we've selected the days that we want to change. If you look at the left hand of the dialogue you'll see that the current setting for the days you've chosen is ⦿ Use default . You can toggle a day as a holiday by clicking on the circle next to ◯ Non-working time .

It's also possible to change from the standard hours of working by clicking on the circle by ○ Non-default working time . Below this circle you see a list of working hours.

◉ Non-default working time	
From:	To:
8:00	12:00
13:00	17:00

Each of these ranges are hours that the resources work. So, for example if you want someone to work from 11am to 12am, then from 1pm to 4pm, then from 4:30pm to 8pm you'd enter

◉ Non-default working time	
From:	To:
11:00	12:00
13:00	16:00
16:30	20:00

Once you've changes these settings and are happy with them you can click OK . The thing you'll notice is that if you've assigned a resource to a task the duration of the task will change depending on the impact of any holidays or non-default days.

Showing Assignments in the Gantt

Sometimes you'll want to show the assignments that have been made to a task. In the Task tab click on Gantt then right click on the bar for the task that you want to show. Choose Show Assignments to see the assignments in the Gantt chart.

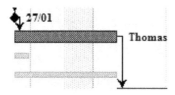

Changing when someone will work on an Assignment

Although someone may be theoretically available to a task for all the time scheduled in their calendar that doesn't always mean that the person can work on the project. For example, someone may need to wait until someone has completed their part of the task.

You can move an assignment in the Gantt chart by clicking and holding the mouse. You'll see the mouse pointer change, and the colour of the bar change also to black.

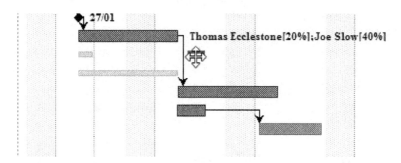

When you let go of the mouse, the assignment will move to the new time. You may also see that the task bar becomes split. This is because no one is working on the project at a particular point in time.

3		Get Finance	6.5 days 27/01/15 16:00	05/0:			Thomas Ecclestone[20%]:Jo
		Joe Slow	1 day 04/02/15 11:00	05/0:			
		Thomas Ecclestone	5 days 27/01/15 16:00	03/0:			
4		Hire Manager	5 days 05/02/15 11:00	12/0:			

Increasing or decreasing assignment duration visually

When you're managing a project it can be useful to visually change settings to see whether some scenario makes sense. This is especially the case with larger projects. To visually increase or decrease assignment length hover your mouse over the end of the bar until it changes to two arrows.

Click and hold the mouse, then drag the bar towards the other side (to reduce the duration of the assignment) or away (to increase it).

While you're changing the bar it'll become hollow, with a black outline.

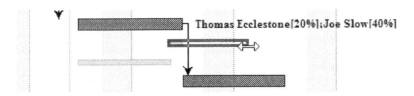

When you let go of the mouse you'll that you've changed the length of time that the individual has been allocated, but you've also changed the duration of the task.

Increasing or decreasing the duration using a Field

Possibly an easier way to change the duration than using the visual method is to just change the duration field in the Gantt chart for that task. Note that durations in the Gantt view are actual days that the employee spends on the task.

Which means that if you change Joe Slow's duration to 6:

			Name	Duration	Start	
1		✓	Write Business Plan	1 day	23/01/15 08:00	23/0
2			Business Plan Complete	0 days	27/01/15 16:00	27/0
3			Get Finance	8.125 days	27/01/15 16:00	06/0
			Joe Slow	*6 days*	*30/01/15 08:00*	*06/c*
			Thomas Ecclestone	*4 days*	*29/01/15 08:00*	*03/c*

Obviously, if required the task duration will change, but the actual hours that Joe Slow will work on the project will lower than the number that is shown in the Gantt chart.

	Name	Work	Work Contour	Assignmen...
1	Thomas Ecclestone	6.4 hours		
	Get Finance	6.4 hours	Flat	1.125 days
2	Joe Slow	19.2 hours		
	Get Finance	19.2 hours	Flat	2.125 days

The Gantt chart reflects the actual physical duration of a task, but each employee will only work on the task a certain percentage of the time.

Find

The find functionality varies depending on the view that you're working in. To find a particular resource, you'd go to the Resources view by clicking on Resource and then Resources. Click into the list of names to select a record. This is a reference point for the Find; you can choose to search above or below the point that you choose.

Click Find to show the Find dialogue box. This dialogue has the option to enter a value to be found:

Find |

Secondly, you can choose to click on the Field combo box in order to see a list of fields to search.

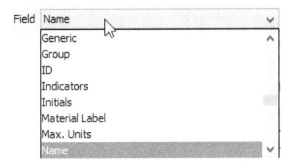

Most of the fields correspond with the header of the columns:

◎	Name	RBS	Type	E-mail Address	Material Label

But there are a lot of other fields. For example Date 1 . These fields which have numbers next to them are Baseline fields.

I'll explain Baselines in more detail later in the book but for now you can think of them as stored values that ProjectLibre can use to compare with the current schedule. For example, you can store the original project baseline when you finish planning the project, and then use it to compare the current schedule and costs with the predicted costs.

To keep it simple I'm going to search for:

To search higher up the list than my current selection I click on  . The field name is highlighted.

	◎	Name	RBS	Type
1	⚙	Thomas Ecclestone		Work
2	⚙	Joe Slow		Work
3	⚙	Samantha Quick		Work

If I were to click 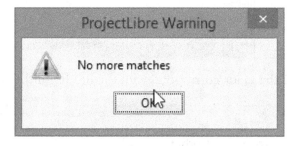 again it would continue searching up the list, and because there are no other items above it with the name Thomas Ecclestone it will display an error message:

You can search down the list (compared to the reference point)

by clicking  .

Alternative Views

So far we've used the basic view for resources. It's possible to use other views, both for Resources and Tasks. These views give you the ability to filter information to an extent.

For example, to see Alternative views for the Resources view

open it up by going to the Resource and then clicking on Resources . At the top left hand corner of the fields table you'll see a large empty square (i.e. the square above the numbers).

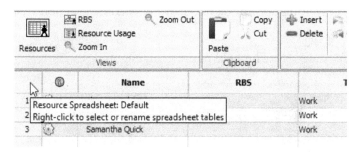

Right click on the square. You'll see a list of alternative views:

		Name
1		Default (Click to rename)
2		Earned Value
3		Earned Value - Cost
		Earned Value - Schedule
		Name

If you click on ___ Name ___ you'll see the table change so that it only contains Names:

	Name
1	Thomas Ecclestone
2	Joe Slow
3	Samantha Quick

You can return to the normal view by right clicking on the square and then default:

	Name	
1	Thomas Ecclestone	
2	Jo	Default
3	Sa	Earned Value
		Earned Value - Cost

Assigned Tasks View

Sometimes you might want to check which tasks have had resources assigned to them, and the amount of assigned resources. In the Task tab click on Task Usage select an alterative view by right clicking on the square at the top left hand corner of the table (i.e. the empty square above the number 1) and then

Tasks Assigned

.

This is the Assigned Task view. You can see the list of tasks that have been assigned, the projected work, actual work, and remaining work. There are other fields such as cost that you can scroll across to view.

	Task	Task ID	Assignment Units	Work	Actual Work	Remainin
1			100%	8 hours	0 hours	8 hc
2			100%	0 hours	0 hours	0 hc
3			20%	10 hours	8 hours	2 hc
	Get Finance	3	20%	8 hours	8 hours	0 hc
	Get Finance	3	100%	2 hours	0 hours	2 hc
4			100%	63 hours	0 hours	63 hc

Assigned Resources

The Assigned Resources view is similar to the Assigned Task resources, in fact it's almost a pivot of the Assigned Task View focusing on resources instead of tasks.

.In the Task tab click on Task Usage and select the alternative view Assigned Resources . The number on the left hand column of this view represents the task, but instead of giving the task and taskID it instead shows the Resource and resource ID.

	Resource	Resource ID	Assignment Units	Work	Actual Work	Remaining ...
1			100%	8 hours	0 hours	8 hours
2			100%	0 hours	0 hours	0 hours
3			20%	10 hours	8 hours	2 hours
	Thomas Ecclestone	1	20%	8 hours	8 hours	0 hours
	Samantha Quick	3	100%	2 hours	0 hours	2 hours
4			100%	63 hours	0 hours	63 hours
5			100%	16 hours	0 hours	16 hours
6			100%	40 hours	0 hours	40 hours

Task Assigned View

You can use this view to see how much of a resources time has been allocated, how much time he has actually spent on the task (Actual Work), and the remaining hours to be spent.

In the  tab click on ▦ Task Usage and select the alternative view Tasks Assigned   .

	Resource	Resource ID	Assignment Units	Work	Actual Work	Remaining ...
1				48 hours	8 hours	40 hours
	Thomas Ecclestone	1	20%	8 hours	8 hours	0 hours
	Thomas Ecclestone	1	50%	0 hours	0 hours	0 hours
	Thomas Ecclestone	1	100%	40 hours	0 hours	40 hours
2				0 hours	0 hours	0 hours
3				2 hours	1 hour	1 hour
	Samantha Quick	3	100%	2 hours	1 hour	1 hour

Note that the number on the left hand side is the resource ID.

Work Vs Actual Work

Well, a number of those alternative views have something interesting in them. There are allocated hours that we've come across so far, but there are also actual hours. When we're working with a task in the Gantt view we often choose to set a task progress indicator to say how far along we are with the task.

But, when we show allocated time so far we haven't indicated how much of the allocated time the employee has used. (I.e. the bar is empty).

The exception to this is that when we indicated that a project is complete, any assignments are also automatically updated to show that they are complete.

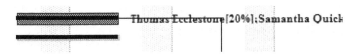

This isn't very useful when you're monitoring a project. If you have an employee who has been assigned 40 hours of work on a task you may want to show how much work he has actually completed. This can show that a project is going over budget. If a project is only

10% complete but the person who has been assigned the project has spent 50% of his or her time on it then you have a problem.

We indicate a resources progress on the project by updating the

Progress field in one of the GANTT views. Click onto the

tab and then the Gantt view. Select the

Tracking alternative view by right clicking on the empty square at the top left hand corner of the table.

Scroll down to the employee and find the task that you want to update:

	Name	Duration	Start	Finish	Percent Complete
1	Write Business Plan	1 day	23/01/15 08:00	23/01/15 17:00	0%
2	Business Plan Complete	0 days	27/01/15 16:00	27/01/15 16:00	0%
3	Get Finance	6.125 days	28/01/15 08:00	05/02/15 09:00	100%
	Thomas Ecclestone	5 days	29/01/15 09:00	05/02/15 09:00	100%
	Samantha Quick	0.25 days	28/01/15 08:00	28/01/15 10:00	10
4	Hire Manager	7.875 days	12/02/15 09:00	23/02/15 17:00	0%
5	Open for Submissions	0 days	05/02/15 08:00	05/02/15 08:00	0%

Once you've done this you'll automatically update the actual work figure, and the progress complete figure in the Gantt chart.

Finding out the Total Cost of your choices so far

To find out the cost of the work completed so far go to the

 tab and click on Projects.

This will show you a summary report with the project name, and summary fields for the entire project as a whole:

Cost	Work	Actual Cost	Actual Work
£312.00	121 hours	£52.00	8.2 hours

Finding out the Cost of particular Task Assignments

In the ⬚ Task tab click on ⬚ Gantt and select the alternative view Cost . This will show you a summary of the costs of the project as a whole, and also the cost of particular assignments to the project and how much of the money has already been spent.

	Name	Cost	Actual Cost	Remaining Cost
1	Write Business Plan	£0.00	£0.00	£0.00
2	Business Plan Complete	£0.00	£0.00	£0.00
3	Get Finance	£68.00	£55.20	£12.80
	Thomas Ecclestone	*£52.00*	*£52.00*	*£0.00*
	Samantha Quick	*£16.00*	*£3.20*	*£12.80*

Resource Usage

Resource Usage shows the actual time that people are assigned to a project. In the ⬚ Resource tab click on ⬚ Resource Usage . You'll see that the screen shows a list of employees and how their time has been allocated on the left hand side of the screen.

	Name	Work	Work Contour	Assignmen...
1	Thomas Ecclestone	48 hours		
	Open for Submissions	*0 hours*	*Flat*	*0 days*
	Read Submissions	*40 hours*		*0 days*
	Get Finance	*8 hours*	*Flat*	*1.125 days*
2	Joe Slow	0 hours		
3	Samantha Quick	2 hours		
	Get Finance	*2 hours*	*Flat*	*0 days*

Plus a chart of when the resources have been allocated on the right hand side.

							26 Jan 15		
	T	W	T	F	S	S	M	T	W
Work	0h	0h	0h	0h	0h	0h	0h	0h	
Work									
Work									
Work									
Work	0h	0h	0h	0h	0h	0h	0h	0h	
Work	0h	0h	0h	0h	0h	0h	0h	0h	
Work									

There are several alternative views to this screen, for example you can see what resources have been assigned to tasks by clicking on **Assigned Resources** .

	Resource	Resource ID	Assignment Units	
1				
	Thomas Ecclestone	1	50%	
	Thomas Ecclestone	1	100%	
	Thomas Ecclestone	1	20%	
2				
3				
	Samantha Quick	3	100%	

Or a list of tasks assigned to a particular employee id. It's worth trying out some of these alternative views to see if they'll be useful to you although I generally just use the resource and assigned resources views.

Next Chapter

In this chapter I've given you a brief look at how to handle Resources in ProjectLibre. You can add, assign, cost, and manage resources easily.

In the next chapter I'm going to discuss ways of recording employee skills so you can more efficiently allocate them to tasks using a third party application

4 RECORDING EMPLOYEE SKILLS

Signing up to Skills Base

First go to the skillsbase website. You may have to google skills-base.com, or type the address into your browser.

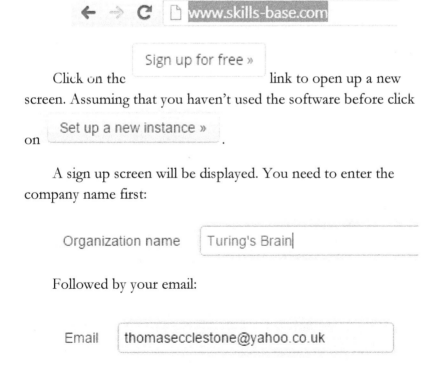

Click on the Sign up for free » link to open up a new screen. Assuming that you haven't used the software before click on Set up a new instance ».

A sign up screen will be displayed. You need to enter the company name first:

Organization name   Turing's Brain

Followed by your email:

Email   thomasecclestone@yahoo.co.uk

Note that this email must be correct. I.e. Skills base will send you an email to verify the account. Finally, you need to give skillsbase a shortcut link that will be the URL that you will use to access skillbase. You can change the default link if you want to.

Shortcut link   http://skills-base.com/o/ | turingsbrain

Click on Check availability as skillsbase checks the address you'll see a progress indicator and then the message Available if the shortcut link is available (otherwise you may have to change the shortcut link).

Next » You'll see a message asking you to confirm the email. Click Yes if the email address is right. You may have a slight pause, with the message:

Waiting for app.skills-base.com...

Followed by:

Please check your email

We have sent an email to:

thomasecclestone@yahoo.co.uk

Go check your email. Depending on the program you use to read your email you should see a new email
like

● Skills Base   Your Skills Base system is ready to go   Your Skills Base instance has been set up an

Open it, read it, and click on the verification link. You'll go to a new screen in your browser:

Create your account

Type in your name:

First Name | Thomas

Surname | Ecclestone

And your password (don't forget to verify it)

Password | ··········

And then agree to the terms and conditions after reading them

Agreement ☑ I have read, and I agree to the terms and conditions .

To create the account click on **Create account** .

Once you've finished you'll see a screen that asks if you want to watch a video or start to add skills. Click on:

Add skills »

Add Skills

Type in the skill name

Skill name | Proofreading

And a description if necessary:

Description [95% accuracy required|] (optional)

Then press **Add skill**. Now, for the first time you'll see the main skills base window.

On the left hand side of the screen is a menu bar. One of the options, skills, is highlighted:

Skills

Note that it's possible to assign skills into categories. At the moment anyone that is added to the skills base will be assessed against all skills. You really want to break this down a bit more so that you're only assessing skills that are relevant to the employee.

Adding Category

Click on 🗀 **New category**. For the moment there aren't any parent categories, so leave

Parent category [(none)   ▼]

As it is. But enter a category name:

Category name [Writing Skills|]

And click on 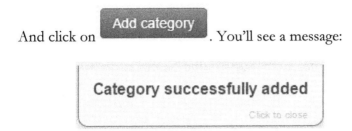. You'll see a message:

Moving an Existing Skill into a new Category

Click on the skill that you want to move and hold the mouse button down. Then drag it to somewhere else in the list. While you're moving it you'll see a big red cross beside it.

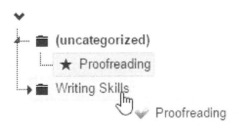

When the mouse is over a category you'll see the cross change to a tick:

When the mouse is over a category you'll see the cross change to a tick:

Let go and the skill will move to the new category. Sometimes, categories are nested so you don't see all the skills that are included in the category:

If this happens click the triangle to the left of the category to expand it.

Adding a New Skill directly to the category

Click on the Category that you want to the skill to:

And then on 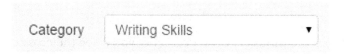. You'll see the Add Skill Form you saw above. The only difference is that there will be a new Category option:

Category	Writing Skills ▼

Check that the category is correct, then add the skill name and description as above.

Skill name	Copyediting
Description	Check document is correct

And naturally click on .

Once you've finished adding all the skills in the category you can click Cancel to go back to the skills directory. Keep on adding categories and skills until you've added all of the skills that you want to record.

Adding People

The next step is that it's fine to have all these skills that you've created, but it's no use for your purposes until you've added some people to the application.

First, in the tab bar to the left hand side of the screen click on People . You'll see a list of people that are already in the application.

Name	Security Group	Self assessment	Supervisor assessment
Thomas Ecclestone	Administrator	Never completed	Never completed

Then, click on ✚ Add people .You have a question to answer at this point, whether you want people to do self-assessments. Personally, I generally think that it is quite a good idea to do so.

Would you like the people you are adding to be able to log in and undertake skill assessments themselves?

Yes   No

So personally, I generally choose yes.

The next screen gives you three options. The third, configure single sign on option is beyond the scope of this book. You can use it to give your employees access to the application through your own login system.

Sending Invitations by email

The first option allows you to send invitation emails out. Click

on **Add people by invitation** You'll get a message telling you

that people will be asked to register themselves and do a self-assessment on the skills that you've set up. Make sure you are happy with the skills set up before you start to add people.

Close

Press to close the warning message.

Now, it's fairly simple. Just add the email addresses one line at a time.

Email addresses: tomterm8@gmail.com

And click on **Send invitations** . Once the invitations have been sent you'll see a message that says:

Invitations sent successfully

Click to close

Responding to an Invitation

Once you've sent your invitations your employee should be sent a message like:

☐ ☆ Skills Base   Thomas Ecclestone has requested you join Skills Base -

They should open the email, read it, and click the verification link. They will see a message headed:

Create your account

Where they can enter their name, password, and agree to the terms just like earlier, and then click on Create account .

Once they've created an account they will have the opportunity to carry out self-assessments.

Self-Assessments

Carry out a self-assessment by clicking Start your self-assessment » . They will see a message like below:

New self-assessment

You are about to begin a new skills self-assessment.

For each skill that is shown, rate your **skill level** and **interest level** based on the descriptions provided in the legend.

Begin the assessment »

And should click on .

They will then be able to fill out their self assesment by clicking on a round circle

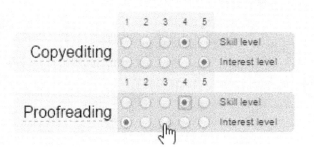

There is a key to the right hand side of the screen which tells you what each choice means.

Click on  when you've filled out the self-assessment. Keep on going until you've filled out all the questions, then there will be a message asking if you are happy with your answers.

Press 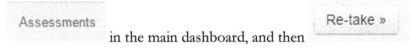 if you are.

Retaking assessments

You can retake an assessment at any time by clicking on

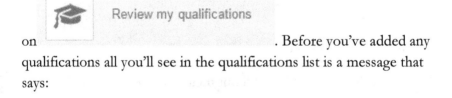 in the main dashboard, and then

Adding Qualifications

To add your qualifications click

on   . Before you've added any qualifications all you'll see in the qualifications list is a message that says:

(There are currently no qualifications assigned)

Click on   and fill in the details of the qualification that you have obtained.

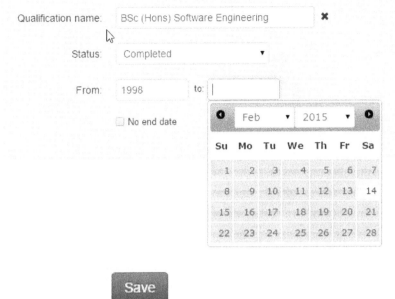

Then click on

Log out

It is important to log out when you finish a session because otherwise security can be compromised. To log out first notice that your user name is at the top right hand corner of the screen.

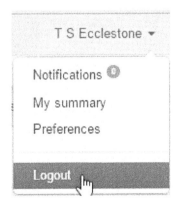

Click on it and then logout.

To log back in, go to your organisations shortcut link (skillsbase will have sent it to you after you created your account) and type your email and password into the fields provided, and then click on

Login

Supervisor Assessments

Click on in the tab bar to the left of the dashboard. This will show a list of people that you can assess.

Name	Supervisor assessment
T S Ecclestone	Never completed

Click on Assess now » to the right of each person that you are managing. You'll have message confirming you are assessing. Begin the assessment.

Begin the assessment »

You can click on the rectangle to see what the person thought themselves.

Show responses from self-assessment

Or just go through the list of skills in the same way as a self-assessment:

When you get to the end check your answers and click . When there are no more assessment questions to answer and as long as you are happy click **Submit**.

You can check the qualifications they've added and their summary page if you want to.

Review T S Ecclestone's qualifications

View T S Ecclestone's summary page

As a supervisor you can edit an employee's qualifications if necessary but this isn't often the case.

Searching for Skills

To find people with the skills that you need use People finder in the tabs on the left hand of the screen. First choose if you want to look for people skilled in or interested in a skill:

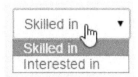

Then choose the skill you want to search for:

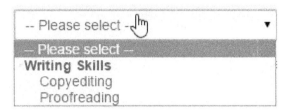

And the competency level required.

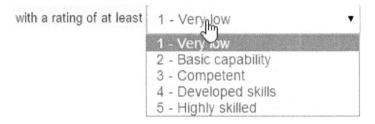

If you want to do a simple skills search the above is fine. If you want something more complicated, click on

➕ Add more criteria to repeat the process. To remove a criteria click on ✖.

When you're happy with your search criteria click on Search to produce a list of matches for your skills.

Exact matches

T S Ecclestone

Copyediting - Skill level: 4.00

Close matches

There are no close matches

Sometimes you might want to control how the skill rating is calculated. Click on Advanced options to choose whether to use supervisor, self or an average rating to determine the search. The default method is to use the average rating..

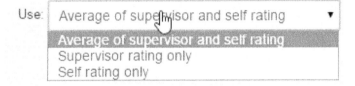

Skills Report

To produce a report of the skills available in your organisation go to Reports in the tab on the left, and then click on **Run report »** to the right of the heat matrix.

You can choose to run the report on specific skill categories

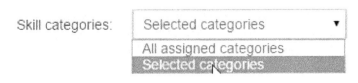

At first, all categories will be selected.

Select categories: ☑ (uncategorized)

☑ Writing Skills

Click on the ☑ to toggle off a category. Finally, choose what kind of ratings to report (average is the default, but you can also run a report of the supervisors ratings or self-ratings)

And press **Run report** to run the report.

Next Chapter

In this chapter I've shown you an application that will help you maintain records of your employee's skills. This should help you when assigning staff to tasks in ProjectLibre.

In the next chapter I'll show you how to use ProjectLibre's reports and views functionality to drill down into project performance.

5 VIEWS AND REPORTS

We've gone into some details already about views in ProjectLibre. As you've seen the default views are only the tip of the iceberg. There are a number of alternative views for both Tasks and Resources but there are also a large number of Reports and Charts that you can use to extract all kinds of information from ProjectLibre.

The View Tab

When you click on the ^{View} tab you'll see two common views:

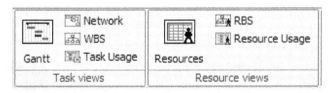

These views are an alternative way of accessing the Gantt and Resources views that we've already seen.

At first it may seem redundant to have these views in the view tab but there's a clue on the other side of the screen.

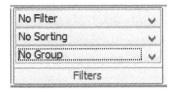

Briefly, you can use the View tab to filter, sort, or group data together allowing you to drill down into the contents of different views. I'll explain it in more detail below. In addition to the Filtering capabilities you can also use Other Views to give you information about the Project, including a summary report, and there is a charts section:

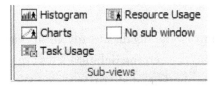

Some of these sub-views are very familiar such as Resource Usage. At the basic level without any filtering, grouping or sorting they are exactly the same views you'd see in the Resource or Task tab.

In addition to the Filtering capacity, though, these views also provide a sub-window at the bottom of the screen that you can use to obtain more information about your selections.

More on Task Views

The Task Views are at the left hand side of the toolbar. They look very familiar. In fact, WBS is identical to the functionality that we've already seen in the Task View. The others allow you more control over the data that's displayed.

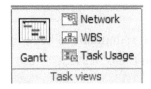

Network

To see a network diagram click 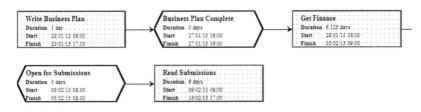 Network . The default setting provides a chart that is the same as the view in the Task Tab:

Write Business Plan		Business Plan Complete		Get Finance
Duration 1 day		Duration 0 days		Duration 6.125 days
Start 23/01/15 08:00		Start 27/01/15 16:00		Start 28/01/15 08:00
Finish 23/01/15 17:00		Finish 27/01/15 16:00		Finish 05/02/15 09:00

Open for Submissions		Read Submissions
Duration 0 days		Duration 8 days
Start 05/02/15 08:00		Start 09/02/15 08:00
Finish 05/02/15 08:00		Finish 18/02/15 17:00

So, what advantage does using the View tab give us? Well, one of the main advantages comes when we decide to filter the Network View. On the Right hand side of the View Tab are the Filter options that I showed earlier. If you click on No Filter ⌄ you'll see a list of different filters:

No Filter ⌄
Filter er ⌃
Completed tasks
Cost overbudget tasks
Critical tasks
In-progress tasks
Incomplete tasks
Late/overbudget tasks
Milestones ⌄

Note that you can continue to scroll down in the list. For example, if you click on Unstarted tasks in the list so the combo box displays Unstarted tasks ⌄ you'll see the tasks in the network diagram restricted by our filter:

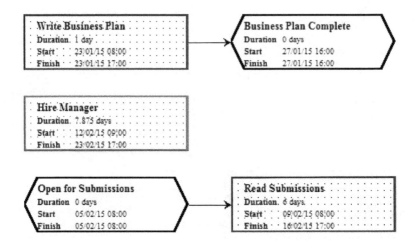

Most of these filter options are pretty obvious. For example, completed tasks, in-progress tasks and so on. There are some filters that seem a bit more unusual. For example the cost overrun filter doesn't make as much sense with regard to what we already know about ProjectLibre.

This is because they refer to a concept called a baseline which I'll explain later, but it's possible for ProjectLibre to handle the idea that there is a planned schedule which then changes as time goes on. Where there are delays in cost or projects are harder to implement than expected a task can go off budget.

In addition to filtering, you can also sort via the sorting **No Sorting** filter, and group the results using the group **No Group** filter. Grouping works much the same way as in a database, combining related records together.

Windows 8.1: There is a known bug that means that some windows 8.1 machines don't handle Sorting or Grouping correctly. If your computer has this bug then when you try to filter by sorting or grouping it won't have any effect on the output window.

In addition to this, you'll find that the filter option becomes ineffective until you close ProjectLibre and open it up again.

This is a problem that I expect the developers will solve at some point, and which doesn't seem to affect all ProjectLibre setups even where they are running on Windows 8.1.

Alternative Views

When you're in the GANTT or the Resource main view you'll find plenty of alternative views that can be useful while you're working on the project.

Baseline

● **Constraint Dates (Click to rename)**

Cost

Default

Earned Value

Earned Value - Cost

Earned Value - Schedule

Name

Opening Publishing Business

Schedule (CPM)

Schedule Variance

Summary

One of the crucial things about accessing these alternative views via the views tab is that you can still filter the results. For example, take the alternative view Cost:

	Name	Cost	Actual Cost
1	Write Business Plan	£0.00	£0.00
2	Business Plan Complete	£0.00	£0.00
3	Get Finance	£68.00	£55.20
4	Hire Manager	£0.00	£0.00
5	Open for Submissions	£0.00	£0.00
6	Read Submissions	£260.00	£0.00

If you were to filter it to In-progress tasks ∨ then you will see only tasks that have started but not been completed:

	Name	Cost	Actual Cost
3	Get Finance	£68.00	£55.20

There are a huge number of filters that you can use which are generally quite self-explanatory.

Charts

Above we discussed ways of filtering alternative views. This produces table views that are very similar to tables that we've already worked with. Such an approach provides the ability to control what information you store and save people from spending a lot of time having to go through all the data in a large project.

Of course, people don't always like looking through large tables of data.

Many people find the idea of a chart to be very helpful when working with data. They can give a visual representation of things that are hard to understand otherwise. To start a chart click on Charts in the sub-views window.

When you start to create a chart you'll see the chart selection window below the main table view.

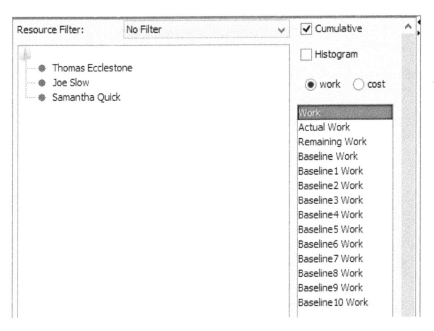

If you're in the GANTT view and select a record where people have been assigned to the task:

You'll see that the Chart selection window changes. The first thing about it is the fact that you have a big round circle next to people who have been assigned the task. ⬡ Thomas Ecclestone

The second thing that you'll notice is that when you select an employee that has been assigned to a task, when you click that employee a chart will appear to the right of the selection window. For example, where you click Get Finance you'll be able to choose an employee name:

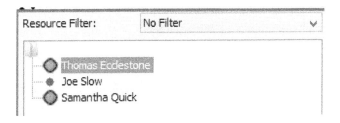

And then you'll see the chart on the right hand side of the screen.

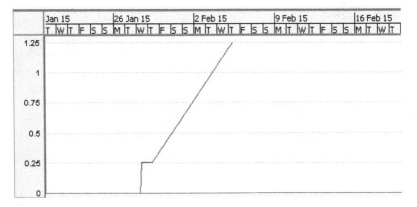

It's possible to change the nature of the chart above. For example, the above chart is a cumulative work chart. I.e. it shows the amount of work that the person will have completed on the project by a particular day.

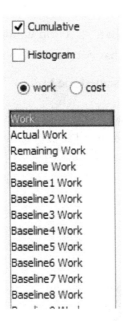

You can change it so the chart is non-cumulative by toggling off

☑ Cumulative in which case you will see a chart of the amount of hours worked on each day of a project:

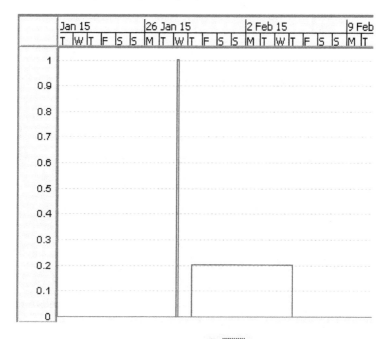

Note that the default option of ⦿ work means that you are only displaying the amount of work that someone has carried out during the life of the project. You can, however, choose to display cost by toggling on ○ cost .

Note that when you do toggle on cost you'll see that the chart immediately changes to the cumulative cost so far:

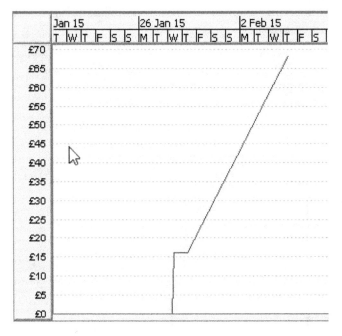

You have quite a number of options. Some of these relate to Baselines, but even at this stage of using projectlibre you'll immediately see some items that are very useful such as

Remaining Cost

Further Filtering and charting multiple tasks

There's one filtering box that is very useful that I haven't shown you so far. This is the resource filter, which is just above the list of filters.

Resource Filter: No Filter

Before you filter the resources you have to click on the task that you want to chart. Remember, to do this click on the number on the left of the chart.

	Name	Cost	Actual Cost
1	Write Business Plan	£0.00	£0.00
2	Business Plan Complete	£0.00	£0.00
3	Get Finance	£68.00	£55.20
4	Hire Manager	£0.00	£0.00
5	Open for Submissions	£0.00	£0.00
6	Read Submissions	£260.00	£0.00

You can select non-contiguous tasks by holding down the control (ctrl) key and then clicking on the number of the next item.

The ability to chart multiple tasks is very useful, where several tasks could be part of the same phase of a project. Sometimes, though, you want to filter the resources in each task more completely, for example so you show people who have not started an assignment yet. To do this you need to activate a resource filter.

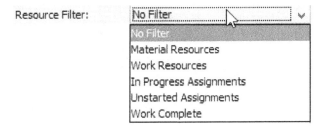

For example if you want to show only people that are involved in unfinished assignments you can do it easily through the resource filter:

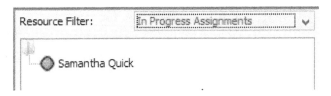

Histograms for Charts

Some people prefer line charts and others prefer histograms. To display a histogram of the chart, click on ☑ Histogram . To display a histogram of the chart options that you have selected.

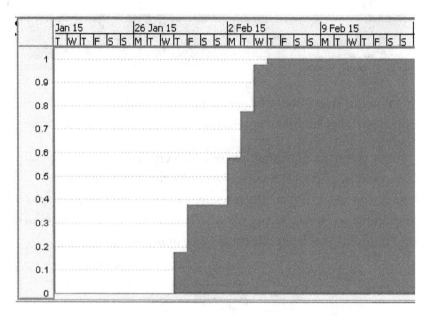

This is one of the things that sometimes people find a bit confusing. There is also a histogram view mode that is a little bit different from the chart view mode. It gives you different filtering options. I'll explain the Histogram View mode below.

Histograms

You can open the Histogram View Mode by clicking on

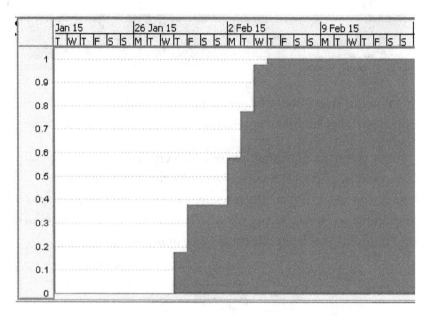 or Histogram in the view tab. The Histogram view mode can be hard to get your head around until you remember to use the alternative view options, and also select different items in your view to chart.

But first, click on . As before, the screen will divide into a top half, and a bottom half. You'll be able to see filtering options on the left:

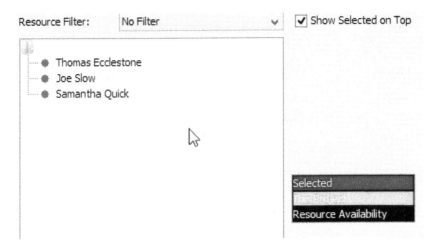

Click on one of the names to select that person:

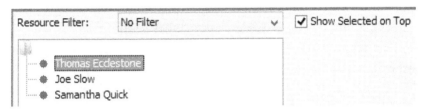

You'll see that there is a histogram that displays the data that you're currently viewing. The key is on the left, but blue is the selected item, green shows this project, and black is total resource availability.

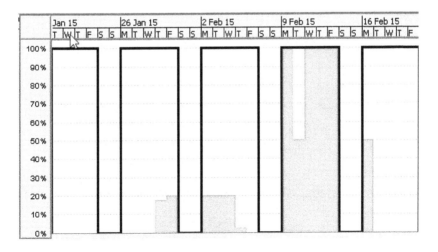

The concept of "Selected" becomes more obvious when you look at the top of the screen. Obviously you can select individual resources using the panel on the left hand side, or particular tasks using the task pane. Either click on the row number or on the column you want to select:

	Name	Work	Duration	Start
1	Write Business Plan	8 hours	1 day	23/01/15 08:00
2	Business Plan Complete	0 hours	0 days	27/01/15 16:00
3	Get Finance	10 hours	6.125 days	28/01/15 08:00
4	Hire Manager	63 hours	7.875 days	12/02/15 09:00
5	Open for Submissions	0 hours	0 days	05/02/15 08:00
6	Read Submissions	40 hours	6 days	09/02/15 08:00

You'll quickly see that the chart changes so that the selected tasks are displayed in blue, allowing you to compare how much time particular tasks require compared to other tasks.

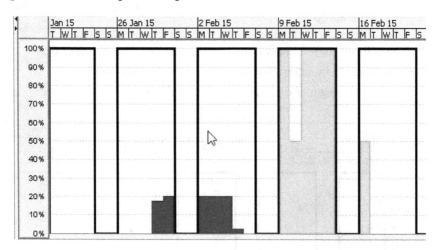

✔ Show Selected on Top

While it's possible to toggle   off I don't recommend that you do it. I think it is almost always very useful to display the selected tasks clearly since it helps you to get an overview of the project.

Saving a Chart

To save a chart right click on the empty square to the left of the dates:

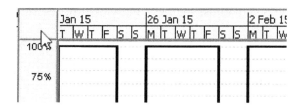

Then click on Save as... . This will open a Save dialogue. Choose the directory, and type in the file name that you want. The chart will be saved as a PNG file when you click Save .

Printing a Chart

Right click on the empty square to the left of the dates as above.

You'll see an Print... option. This unfortunately doesn't give you access to a print preview. Instead you'll see a page setup dialogue that allows you to control the Paper format, i.e. whether it is A4 or US Letter) and the tray if appropriate.

You can also choose whether the document should be printed out as Portrait or Landscape. Personally, I often think that Landscape is better than Portrait even though it isn't the default choice.

Finally, you can adjust the page margins if necessary:

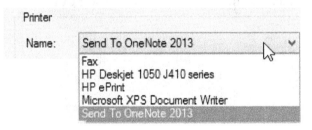

Once you click [OK] ProjectLibre will bring up a Print dialogue that allows you to control which Printer to print to:

Printer

Name: Send To OneNote 2013 ⌄
Fax
HP Deskjet 1050 J410 series
HP ePrint
Microsoft XPS Document Writer
Send To OneNote 2013

As well as the print range and how many copies that you want to print.

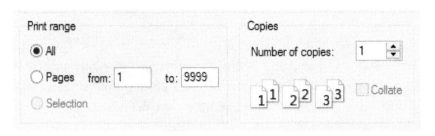

When you're happy with your choices click on OK .

Report

To generate a report click on Report in the View tab. You will see a print preview of a summary report for the project. Just above the preview of the report is a combo box which allows you to choose the kind of report that you want to produce.

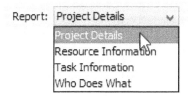

Some of the reports have the ability to control what columns are printed in the report. For example, you can choose to print out Earned Value or cost in the Resource Information report.

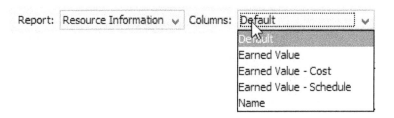

It's worth experimenting with columns to see if there is a report that covers exactly what you want to find out.

Click on to print the report. You'll see a print dialogue with the same options I discussed earlier under printing a Chart. Or press to save the report. By default the report is saved as a JasperReport format file, but many windows users won't have this software installed so I would suggest that you click on the Files of Type combo box and select one of the other formats. I find that excel format (XLS) is good for most windows users, or if you don't mind if you can edit it PDF.

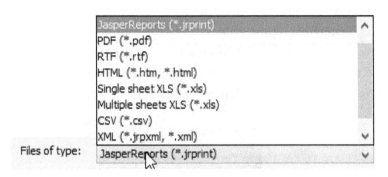

The rest of the save as dialogue Is standard.

Clearing the sub-views

To hide the current sub-view click on No sub window in the View tab. While the sub view will close, you'll be able to open it again from the sub-view options in the View tab.

Next Chapter

In this chapter I've detailed how to produce reports and charts in ProjectLibre. These reports allow you to monitor the progress, cost and progress of your Project accurately.

The next chapter will go further, explaining the concept of baselines so that you can create a basic plan and then see how the project is deviating from it over time.

6 BASELINES

Baselines are a technique that ProjectLibre uses to allow you to compare actual progress and planned progress. When using ProjectLibre you have two main phases during a project:

- Project Planning – where you're creating tasks, assigning resources, and deciding how long the tasks should take and,
- Project Implementation – where you're actually carrying out the project.

Everyone's heard the saying "the best laid plans of mice and men," and the reality is that project planning almost deviates from the actual reality.

When using baselines, there are two major phases. We've effectively covered the first phase – creating the project plan. The second phase starts once you've saved the baseline.

Saving a Baseline

In the File tab click on Save Baseline . You'll see the Save Baseline dialogue.

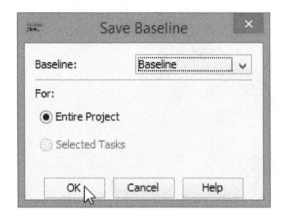

By default if you want to save the baseline for the entire project you can click on 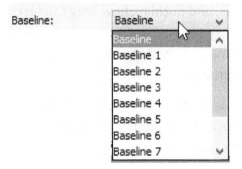. If you click on the word Baseline you'll see that you can actually record more than one baseline. There are reports that you can do on different baselines but I find that in most of the projects that I've worked on just using the Baseline and Actual performance is generally enough for myself.

You don't have to save the entire project as a baseline. You can just save selection of tasks. To do this before clicking on Save Baseline

go to the Task tab and click on Gantt to go into the Gantt view. Then select the tasks that you want to save by either dragging the mouse along the numbers, or holding down control (ctrl) and clicking the number of each task that you want to select.

		Name	Duration	Start	
1		Write Business Plan	1 day	23/01/15 08:00	23/0
2		Business Plan Complete	0 days	27/01/15 16:00	27/0
3		Get Finance	6.125 days	28/01/15 08:00	05/0
4		Hire Manager	7.875 days	12/02/15 09:00	23/0
5		Open for Submissions	0 days	05/02/15 08:00	05/0
6		Read Submissions	6 days	09/02/15 08:00	16/0

Then go to the File tab and press Save Baseline . This will bring up the Save Baseline dialogue that you saw earlier. One difference is that you will see selected tasks is no longer greyed out in the dialogue:

For:

⦿ Entire Project

◯ Selected Tasks

If you click it to toggle it on ⦿ Selected Tasks then ProjectLibre will save the baseline only for the particular tasks.

Why's this important? Say you're in the implementation phase. You have created a baseline for the project. You don't want to change the baseline for the tasks that you've already completed but, because you're agile, you want to change tasks that are going to happen in the future. As you change the tasks that exist in the future you can save the baseline but only for those individual task.

Clearing a baseline

First, decide if you want to delete the baseline for a particular task or the entire project. If you want to delete the baseline for a particular set of tasks you'll need to select them by going to the

Task then pressing Gantt for the Gantt view. Select the tasks to remove by dragging the mouse along the numbers or holding down control (ctrl) and clicking the number for each task you want to

select.

Once you've selected the tasks (if necessary) or if you just want to clear the baseline for all the tasks click Clear Baseline in the

File tab. This will bring up the Clear Baseline Task dialogue. Just like when you are saving a baseline the first thing to do is to decide which baseline to clear. Click on the Baseline combo box and select the baseline that you want to clear.

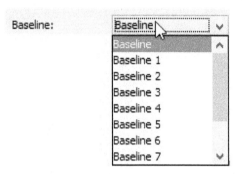

If you have selected tasks you'll see that neither of the for options is greyed out.

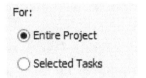

To clear the baseline for the entire project leave the default option as ⦿ Entire Project otherwise toggle Selected Tasks on by clicking on the circle ◯ Selected Tasks so that it shows ⦿ Selected Tasks .

Once you've chosen your options and as long as you're happy with them click on OK .

Using the Baseline

Once you've saved the baseline you'll find that not much appears to have changed within the application. You can still assign resources, change duration, and so on just like before.

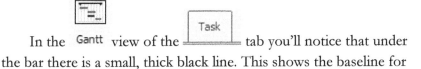

In the Gantt view of the Task tab you'll notice that under the bar there is a small, thick black line. This shows the baseline for the task.

You can still increase or decrease the duration of a task in the same way as before, by either changing the field or using the mouse and dragging the task bar so it's longer or shorter.

One thing to notice is that when you change the duration, there are obvious markers that tell you that the duration has changed from the baseline. The line under the bar is shorter in this instance than the new duration. And there is a blue line in the middle of the bar that shows you when the task has been completed.

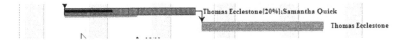

One of the disadvantages of ProjectLibre is that it doesn't clearly show when you change the assigned resources of a project. This might seem a minor matter but it can have cost implications since different people can have different hourly wages.

Basically, though, you can make any change to a task where you've saved a baseline as a task where you haven't saved a baseline.

The value of the baseline becomes more obvious when you start to look at the reports and chars that we've used in the last chapter.

For example, click on ▦ Report in the View tab. You'll see that the report includes the baseline, and actual hours worked:

Work			
Scheduled	235.263 hours	Remaining	194.863 hours
Baseline	137 hours	Actual	40.4 hours

As well as the Baseline costs, and the actual cost, and variance.

Costs			
Scheduled	£1607.11	Remaining	£1343.91
Baseline	£841.00	Actual	£263.20
		Variance	-£230.62

Obviously, this report is just the summary report for the project.

But we can use the baseline in a more advanced way from the View tab. We've just made changes to the Get Finance task, so let's see how we can use the chart views to see the effect of those changes.

First, select the task that you want to chart by pressing Gantt in the View tab and clicking on the task's number.

	ⓘ	Name	Duration	Start	
1		Write Business Plan	1 day	23/01/15 08:00	23/0
2		Business Plan Complete	0 days	27/01/15 16:00	27/0
3		Get Finance	9.166 days	28/01/15 08:00	10/0
4		Hire Manager	9.875 days	12/02/15 09:00	25/0:
5		Open for Submissions	0 days	05/02/15 08:00	05/0:
6		Read Submissions	6 days	09/02/15 08:00	16/0:

Then press ▦ Charts in the sub-views options. You'll see the chart view open up. In the Resource View box click on all the resources that you want to produce a chart for. In this case, it's all of them.

So far, the steps have been broadly the same as he had before. And we still have to decide if we want to use a Histogram chart, or make the chart cumulative or non-cumulative.

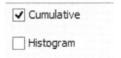

As well as choosing whether we're going to chart work or cost .

The real difference comes in the next stage. Deciding what to chart. In the last chapter, to show the cost we'd have just used either Cost, or Actual cost.

Which would produce a chart like the following:

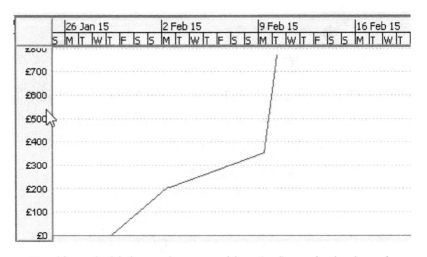

But if you hold down the control key (ctrl) on the keyboard, you can also click on baseline cost:

Which produces a chart that compares the cost with the Baseline Cost:

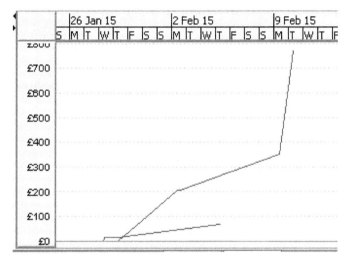

(These chart lines are different colours: cost is in red, and baseline cost is in black. When you select the variables to chart you'll see that the highlight colour is the same as the line colour for the variable).

Seeing the Baseline vs Actual work in Task Usage

So far we've seen how we can chart baseline vs real work in the charts and histograms. But there are several other views where it's very useful to be able to compare the difference.

For example, click on Gantt in the View tab then select the task that you want to view task usage for.

2		Business Plan Complete	0 days 27/01/15 16:00	27/0
3		Get Finance	9.166 days 28/01/15 08:00	10/0
4		Hire Manager	9.875 days 12/02/15 09:00	25/0

Then click on Task Usage to show the task usage side panel:

107

	Name	Work		26 Jan 15				
				M	T	W	T	F
3	Get Finance	108.263 hours	Work			8h	15h	16h
	Samantha Quick	25.727 hours	Work			8h	8h	8h
	Thomas Ecclestone	64.329 hours	Work				7h	8h
	Joe Slow	18.207 hours	Work					

Right click on the empty square next to the date to show the fields that the table will display.

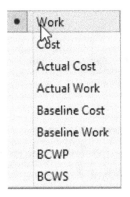

●	Work
	Cost
	Actual Cost
	Actual Work
	Baseline Cost
	Baseline Work
	BCWP
	BCWS

Click on Baseline Work to include the field in the table. You'll be able to compare the work on each day by each member of staff with the actual work done.

	Name	Work		26 Jan 15					
				M	T	W	T	F	S
3	Get Finance	108.263 hours	Work			8h	15h	16h	
			Basel...			2h	1.4h	1.6h	
	Samantha Quick	25.727 hours	Work			8h	8h	8h	
			Basel...			2h			
	Thomas Ecclestone	64.329 hours	Work				7h	8h	
			Basel...				1.4h	1.6h	
	Joe Slow	18.207 hours	Work						
			Basel...						

Note that from the above char you're not limited to just work. You can also show the baseline cost Vis cost, or the predicted cost vs the actual cost so far and so on.

Resource Usage

Above we dealt with Task Usage but it won't come as a surprise to you that you can use the same technique in the resource usage view. First, select the task that you want to show resource usage for as above.

	⚓	Name	Duration
1	▣	Write Business Plan	1 da
2	▣	Business Plan Complete	0 day
3	▣	Get Finance	9.166 day
4	▣	Hire Manager	9.875 day

Then click on 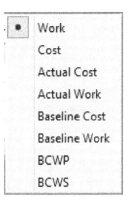 Resource Usage . You'll see the normal resource usage sub view window appear:

	Name	Work			2 Feb 15					
					M	T	W	T	F	S
1	Thomas Ecclestone	183.329 hours	Work		8h	8h	8h	8h	8h	
	Read Submissions	40 hours	Work							
	Get Finance	64.329 hours	Work		8h	8h	8h	8h	8h	
	Open for Submissions	0 hours	Work						0h	
	Hire Manager	79 hours	Work							

Right click on the empty square next to the date to show the fields that you want to display.

- ● Work
- Cost
- Actual Cost
- Actual Work
- Baseline Cost
- Baseline Work
- BCWP
- BCWS

Then click on baseline work. You'll see the Baseline vs the actual work in the view.

	Name	Work		2 Feb 15					
				M	T	W	T	F	S
1	Thomas Ecclestone	183.329 hours	Work	8h	8h	8h	8h	8h	0h
			Basel...	1.6h	1.6h	1.6h	0.2h	0h	0h
	Read Submissions	40 hours	Work						
			Basel...						
	Get Finance	64.329 hours	Work	8h	8h	8h	8h	8h	
			Basel...	1.6h	1.6h	1.6h	0.2h		
	Open for Submissions	0 hours	Work					0h	
			Basel...					0h	
	Hire Manager	79 hours	Work						
			Basel...						

As we've seen, baselines are a very easy to use, simple feature. But they are more powerful than they seem. As you work on a project the ability to see how some people are doing more work than expected, and others are doing less helps guide you when you produce future project plans.

So Long and Thanks

I've enjoyed working on this book and I hope that you have enjoyed reading it. ProjectLibre is a powerful program, especially when you combine it with TimeTracker and SkillsBase. I hope that I've shown you how to use them to give you a powerful project management system.

You can contact me at thomasecclestone@yahoo.co.uk if you have any questions or comments about the book.

I hope that you enjoy using ProjectLibre, and get a lot out of using it when you're managing your projects.

ABOUT THE AUTHOR

Thomas Ecclestone is a software engineer and technical writer who lives in Kent, England. After getting his 1st class honours in software engineering he worked at the National Computing Centre in Manchester, the Manchester Metropolitan University, and for BEC systems Integration before starting his own business in software development. He is a writer who lives on a smallholding in Kent where he looks after a small flock of Hebridean sheep.

www.ingramcontent.com/pod-product-compliance
Lightning Source LLC
Chambersburg PA
CBHW071255050326
40690CB00011B/2411